Walks in the Rhubarb Triangle

Richard Bell

with recipes by Barbara Bell

Contents

Willow Island Editions

Marooned in the Rhubarb Triangle

BARBARA & I usually zip across the **Rhubarb Triangle** on the M1 from Wakefield to Leeds in 5 or 10 minutes but one day the clutch cable snapped on our car.

As we waited for the road-side rescue, I sketched the view. Traffic thundered by on one side, while on the other there was a peaceful scene of rhubarb fields and forcing sheds. A farmer drove his tractor through the field followed by a black and white cat.

We hope that these walks, stories and recipes will give you a taste of the 'hidden' countryside of the Rhubarb Triangle.

Access: for the most part these walks follow public and permissive rights of way or cross public parks and open spaces but diversion orders can be made and permissions withdrawn. We cannot of course be held responsible for such diversion orders and any inaccuracies in the text which result from these or any other changes to the routes nor any damage which might result from walkers trespassing on private property. In one case *(page 30)*, as mentioned in the text, we came across a blockage to a public footpath. Please take care when finding your way around such obstructions and look for any new way-marking that might have appeared since we checked out the walks. We'd be grateful if you would let us know about any changes to routes by e-mailing us: **richard@willowisland.co.uk**

Most of these walks can be muddy in places.

Map: OS Explorer 278 Leeds

Waterways: part of the towpath alongside the Calder & Hebble Navigation at Thornes Flood Locks is not a public right of way but British Waterways encourage its leisure use. Always take special care of children when visiting waterways and towing paths, particularly near locks.

Acknowledgements: my thanks to the **Countryside Service** and **footpaths officers** of **Wakefield Metropolitan District Council** and the **footpaths officer** of **Leeds City Council**. Thank you to the staff of **Wakefield Visitor Centre** for their enthusiasm. We are grateful to **Heather Gardner** for testing the rhubarb cheesecake recipe and to **John Gardner** *(www.johngardner.co.uk)* for his mouthwatering photograph of it.

Also by Richard Bell

All Sorts of Walks in Liquorice Country
Walks in Robin Hood's Yorkshire
Walks around Horbury
Walks around Newmillerdam
Walks around Ossett
Thornes Park
Sandal Castle
Wakefield Words
Drawing on Reserves
Rough Patch - a sketchbook from the wilder side of the garden

Please keep in single file as you cross fields and *don't* be tempted to nibble the raw rhubarb!

ISBN 978-1-902467-18-4
Third edition with revisions
© Richard Bell 2013
www.willowisland.co.uk
41 Water Lane, Middlestown, Wakefield, West Yorkshire, WF4 4PX

A Brief History of Rhubarb

Rhubarb thrives with cold winters and in rich, moist soil . . .

Southern Siberia, 30,000 years ago . . .

Oxalic acid and other chemicals give rhubarb a defence against grazing animals

China, 2,700 years ago; dried powdered rhubarb root is regarded as a powerful medicine.

1227: Genghis Khan's men bring two camel-loads of rhubarb back from China.

*c.*1275: **Marco Polo** visits the mountains of Tangut, China.

Rhubarb is found in great abundance

When it arrives in Europe, rhubarb is prized as a medicine.

It is under the dominion of Mars . . . It is good against venomous bites.
Nicholas Culpeper, 1653

In Victorian gardens, rhubarb becomes popular as a 'fruit' to fill in the gap between the last of the apples and the first of the raspberries.

Buckets, pots or barrels are used to 'force' an earlier crop.

1877: In commercial growing, after exposure to the cold, roots are taken into forcing sheds and grown on in the warmth by candlelight.

A special night train from Ardsley Station carried 200 tons of rhubarb to London until 1966.

Rabarbaro Zucca is an Italian aperitif made from rhubarb.

There's a statue to rhubarb in Wakefield's Thornes Park.

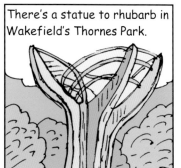

See page 25

Prophet Wroe's Mansion

MELBOURNE HOUSE gets its name because, working without any plans, **Prophet Wroe** *(see page 6)* is said to have based his mansion, built 1856-57, on old Melbourne Town Hall. Some of Wroe's followers believed that 144,000 elect of the Lost Tribes of Israel would gather here to await the Apocalypse.

The four **entrance lodges,** originally one at each corner of the grounds, may have had symbolic significance; when Wroe was involved in building the Christian Israelite Sanctuary in Ashton-under-Lyne in 1825, four 'Gates to the Temple' (actually large brick-built villas) were built at the four corners of the town.

Notice on the wall by the gates; others warned 'BEWARE MAN-TRAPS!'. After Wroe's death, New York businessman turned prophet **'Judge' Daniel Milton** *(1821-1903)* attempted to claim the house, pasting posters on these walls and even bringing his step-ladder so he could peer over them into grounds.

The grounds were planted with shrubs, fruit trees and flowers. There were hot-houses, conservatories and this **grotto** where Wroe would sit for many hours meditating.

Aspen Farm, Kirkhamgate

Old Melbourne Farm

Growers of Yorkshire rhubarb since 1870

In early summer look for **Meadow Foxtail**, a tall grass of meadows and verges. The soft silvery sausage-shaped flower-spikes are given a foxy appearance by the reddish anthers *(point 4 to 5).*

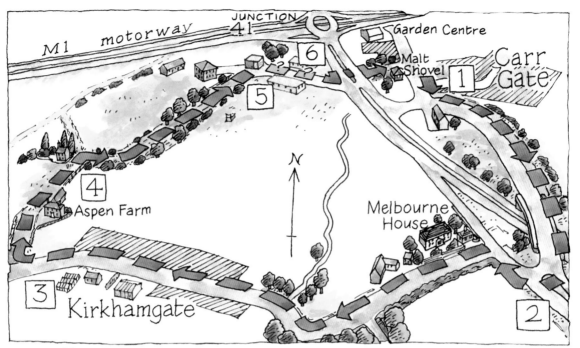

Melbourne House

1½ miles, 2.5 km., 45 minutes

Parking: near the **Malt Shovel** public house on the old **Bradford Road**, Carr Gate, off the A650 south of junction 41 on the M1

Buses: 425, 427, 481   **OS ref:** SE 311240

1. With the **Malt Shovel** public house on your right, walk back to the end of the road. Turn left at the give way sign (note **Carr Gate war memorial** on your right) and follow the curving road, which soon takes you on a bridge over the **A650** Wakefield to Bradford road.

2. After the bridge, just past the junction on your right, cross at the dimpled, drop-curb crossing point, head towards the stone-built gate lodge then turn left onto **Brandy Carr Road**, signed to 'Kirkhamgate 1¼'. After passing **Melbourne House, Old Melbourne Farm** and **The Granary** (c.1650, rebuilt 1990), the road crosses a small stream as you enter the village of **Kirkhamgate**.

3. After 350 yards, you pass **Brandy Carr Nurseries** on your left then, 80 yards after the last cottage (no. 207 Brandy Carr Road) on your right, turn right on a public footpath signed to East Ardsley, which follows the tarmacked driveway to **Aspen Farm**. The footpath continues through a squeeze-through stile just as you come to the iron gates of the farm.

4. Continue down a little farm track towards an isolated cottage on your left, after which you pass through a kissing gate at the foot of the slope. Turn right on a path that follows a grassy ribbon through shrubs and trees which takes you past the police stables and dog training establishment on your left.

5. When the footpath emerges at the police training college (under construction at the time of writing) turn right to reach the dual carriageway but please look out for any new access arrangements.

6. Taking great care, cross the dual carriageway at the refuge, then turn right and immediate left on a public footpath along a lane, emerging back near the start of the walk, near the Malt Shovel Inn.

Prophet Wroe

John Wroe, 1782-1863

2 A.M., 12ᵗʰ November, 1819: in fields near Tong Street, Bradford, wool-comber John Wroe has the first of his visions...

'I thought I walked about a mile with running oxen...

'An angel met me. I saw large altars and a great number of books.'

Wroe becomes a preacher and prophet

Declare ye among the nations!

1.30 p.m. Sunday 29ᵗʰ February, 1824: 30,000 gather to see Wroe's baptism in the River Aire at Apperley Bridge.

But part of the riverbank collapses casting several jeering young men into the water...

A riot ensues!

1825: in Ashton-under-Lyne the Christian Israelites build a Sanctuary...

Welcomed as their prophet, Wroe takes seven virgins from the congregation on his preaching tours...

After allegations of mis-conduct he leaves. His preaching tours take him round the world...

NEW YORK 1840

SYDNEY 1843

HOBART 1850

NIAGARA FALLS 1859

1854: Wroe announces that the Lord has com-manded him to build a 'temple'...

the donations flood in!

Whit Sunday 1857: followers from all over the world join their prophet – now 75 – at the opening cere-mony at Melbourne House.

5ᵗʰ February 1863: Wroe dies at the Christian Israelites' Sanctuary at Fitzroy, Melbourne, Australia. His followers keep his room at Mel-bourne House ready for their prophet's return.

THEY LEAVE HIS SLIPPERS AT HIS BEDSIDE

Rhubarb Triangles

The rhubarb contrasts with the sweetness of this flapjack and gives it a moist texture.

makes 16 triangles

150g butter
30g soft brown sugar
3 generous tablespoons
golden syrup
275g rolled oats
2 teaspoons ground ginger
100g fresh rhubarb cut into
small dice

Grease and line the base of a 17 x 27cm baking tin.

Place butter, sugar and golden syrup into a large saucepan and melt over a gentle heat, taking care not to burn.

Remove from heat and stir in the remaining ingredients. Tip into the prepared baking tin, levelling out with the back of a spoon.

Place in a pre-heated oven at 190°C (375°F, gas mark 5) and bake for 20 to 25 minutes or until golden.

While still warm cut into triangles. Cool in the tin.

Rhubarb Cheesecake

A rhubarb version of the classic baked cheesecake.

serves 6

175g digestive biscuits
crushed to fine crumb
50g butter
500g diced rhubarb
175g caster sugar
500g mascarpone cheese
2 tablespoons cornflour
3 medium eggs

Preheat the oven to 180°C (350°F gas mark 4). Grease and line the base of a 20cm loose-based or spring-form baking tin with baking parchment.

Put the diced rhubarb and 100g of the sugar in a pan and poach gently, stirring occasionally for about 5 to 10 minutes until the rhubarb is tender. Strain through a sieve (you can reserve the juice to pour over the cheesecake if you wish).

Melt the butter and stir in the crushed biscuits then press down firmly in the tin. Chill the base while you make the topping.

Whisk together the mascarpone, cornflour, eggs and remaining sugar until smooth. Fold in the rhubarb then pour into the tin.

Bake for 40 minutes until set but still with a slight wobble. Cool in the tin. Serve with cream or crème fraîche and reserved juice if desired.

Photograph: www.johngardner.co.uk

Lawns Village

Parking: near **Carr Gate Garden Centre** on the old **Bradford Road** off the A650, south of the M1, junction 41. **Buses:** 425, 427, 481 **OS ref.:** SE 310244

1. With your back to the garden centre, take the public footpath to the east across the field. If there's a crop in the field the path might not be obvious so please look for any way-marking, keep in single file and head immediately to the

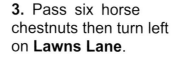

right of a large tree on the far side of the field, to the right of the tall Lombardy poplars (to give you some idea of the direction, the blue south-bound motorway junction sign should be directly behind you in the distance).

2. Go through the metal kissing gate and, for a short while, follow the left-hand side of a pasture, with a hedge on your left. After 30 yards, go through a second gate and follow the fenced-in path with the hedgerow on your right. You'll cross another stile before emerging at the end of a driveway.

3. Pass six horse chestnuts then turn left on **Lawns Lane**.

4. After walking 300 yards along the lane, turn left on the footpath signed **East Ardsley ¾**, which takes you along a track and up on a footbridge over the motorway.

5. After crossing the motorway, continue directly ahead on a farm track then keep on up the slope on a footpath with a hedgerow on your right.

6. When you reach the oak at the corner of the copse on your left, turn right on a footpath over the fields. *From this track on a clear day you can see as far as Eggborough and Drax power stations, 16 and 21 miles to the east.*

7. After crossing the fields you join a narrow field lane (**Stubbs Lane**). Turn left for 50 yards then right on the road (**Cave Lane**) downhill with the houses, including **Moss Grove Cottages** *(1887)* on your right.

8. The lane peters out and when you reach a large block of sandstone continue through the small wooden gate ahead of you. Follow the track until you reach a pond then, ignoring a metal kissing gate on your right, continue on the track past the lower end of the pond.

9. Soon after entering the wood, **Spring Lane Sidings**, turn right along the old tarmacked lane.

10. When you emerge on **Lingwell Gate Lane**, turn right under the motorway bridge, and in 100 yards take the turning, back onto Lawns Lane, on your right.

11. Stay on this lane, re-entering **Lawns** village at **Trevor Terrace**. In a quarter of a mile, after **Sunnyside**, number 31, and immediately after a lane *(Grand Stand Road, site of Outwood racecourse until 1794)* on the left, turn right at the row of horse chestnuts to retrace your steps to the start of this walk.

Lawns Village

THE PLACE NAME **Lawns** or 'Laundes' suggests a glade at the edge of a wood where deer might graze. Wakefield's **Outwood**, some 2,500 acres (1000 hectares) in extent was so thick and extensive in Elizabethan times that a guide was employed to show travellers through.

The Forest of Leeds *initiative aims to integrate trees and woodland with urban areas.*

'Stubbs' in Stubbs Lane probably refers to a cleared area with tree stumps.

I'm told that the old schoolroom (point 10) was once used as a toffee factory. For many years the toffees made here were sold on a stall on Wakefield market. The bell is cracked.

The West Yorkshire Railway between Wakefield Westgate and Leeds opened in 1857 and was acquired by the **Great Northern Railway** in 1865. The **M1 motorway** - including junction 42 - was built in 1966 but the M62 didn't come along until seven years later.

1297: Adam Hood, who is thought to have been the father of **Robert Hode** *(also known as Robin Hood), was a forester, responsible for protecting the lord of the manor's deer (see my **Walks in Robin Hood's Yorkshire**).*

Wild flowers in early summer: *(left to right)* **Green Alkanet, Garlic Mustard, Bluebell, Meadow Buttercup**

Roman coins, coin-moulds and crucibles have been found around here *(point 9 to 10 on the walk)* since 1697. The brass coins resemble dinarii and were struck between AD 138 and 278. There may have been an official mint here coining money for the legions.

The name **alkanet** comes from the Arabic name for henna as the plant, especially the roots, can be boiled to produce a cherry red dye, used by the Victorians in lip balm. A native of south-west Europe, it was grown in cottage gardens and it can still be seen at Lawns village.

Lingwell Gate was an entrance to the Outwood. Lingwell was the only place in the parish of Lofthouse where **ling** (heather) grew. This gate *(left, at point 10)* incorporates a cast iron wheel.

In the 18th century the spectre of the **Green Lady of Lawns** was said to walk the terraces and grandstand of **Outwood Racetrack** when night fell.

Stanley Marsh

These **cottages**, at the end of Lime Pit Lane, were once the offices of the **Victoria Mining Company**. On 4th March 1879 there was a firedamp (methane) explosion beneath the Stanley Marsh area in the **Deep Drop Pit**, then the property of R. Hudson & Co.. Twenty-one mineworkers were killed. The youngest, James Dolan, aged 12, worked with pit ponies.

In August 1839, during the construction of George Leather's 1,700 ton, 50 metre long cast iron **Stanley Aqueduct**, an oak **logboat** 18 feet long was found. Carbon dating suggests that it was in use - probably to ferry passengers across the river - around the year 1000 A.D.. It has been kept at the **Yorkshire Museum** since 1840.

Ramsdens Bridge, the swing bridge below the modern footbridge, has a stone-built keeper's cottage alongside.

Stanley Hall, now Wakefield Hospice, was built in 1802 by Wakefield cloth-merchant **Benjamin Heywood**

Clarke Hall *was built by* **Benjamin Clarke** *in c. 1680.*

Stanley Ferry Flash, which formed because of mining subsidence is fringed with reed and reedmace, more commonly known as 'bulrush'.

At the dissolution of **St Swithin's Chantry** (point 7) in 1548, its two bells were taken to the Chantry Chapel on Kirkgate Bridge. In medieval times a hermit occupied the chapel which lay at the edge of Wakefield's Old (deer) Park.

Harts-tongue Fern (left) on a wall near the Aberford Road roundabout, **wild carrot** *at Stanley Ferry Flash*

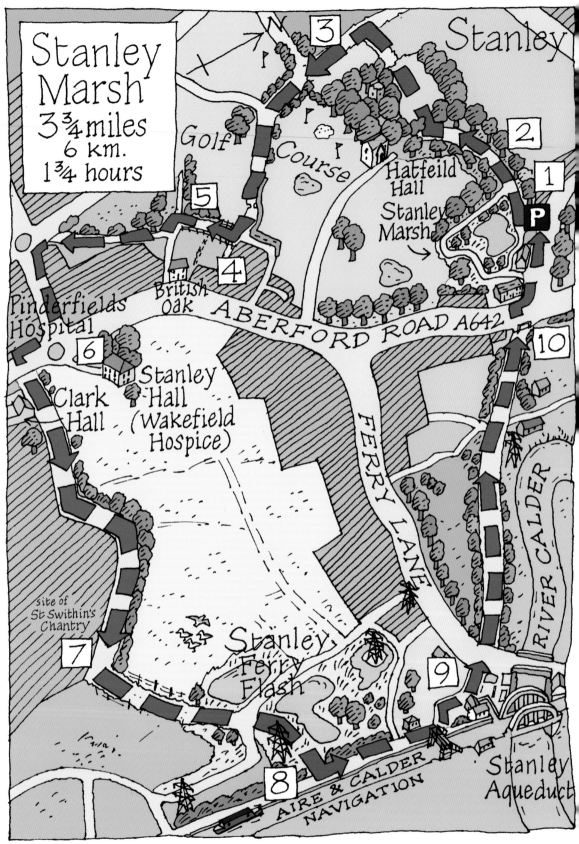

Stanley
Marsh
3¾ miles
6 km.
1¾ hours

Stanley

Golf
Course

Hatfeild
Hall
Stanley
Marsh

P

Pinderfields
Hospital

British
Oak

ABERFORD ROAD A642

Stanley
Hall
(Wakefield
Hospice)

Clark
Hall

FERRY LANE

RIVER CALDER

Site of
St Swithin's
Chantry

Stanley
Ferry
Flash

Stanley
Aqueduct

AIRE & CALDER NAVIGATION

Stanley Marsh

Parking: Stanley Marsh car park, Lime Pit Lane, Stanley
Buses: 125,147, 157, 444, X41
OS ref.: SE 346237

1. Go through the gate at the back of the car park and bear right on the broad track with the marsh on your left.

2. Ignoring the path on your left, leave the reserve via the metal kissing gate on the permissive footpath ahead through an avenue of trees. As this path curves to the left towards **Hatfeild Hall**, take the permissive footpath between the ivy-covered trees on your right. Cross the grassy space towards a gate in the top left-hand corner and continue ahead across a field then turn left at a T-junction with a footpath.

3. Follow this footpath down the open slope, cross a railway sleeper bridge and continue ahead on a path between hedges. When you reach a bend on a track, **Finkin Lane**, follow it ahead to the left, ignoring turns to left and right onto the golf course. In 50 yards follow the old stone wall on your left, leaving the golf course via a final kissing gate.

4. In 200 yards, when Finkin Lane turns sharply to the left, take the footpath ahead on your right for 50 yards then take the path on your right which runs up the slope between fences with paddocks on your left and a small copse on the right.

5. In 200 yards turn left then in 40 yards right to follow a footpath up the slope with trees on your right and, after 200 yards, the backs of houses on your left. In another 250 yards, when you emerge at Pinderfields Hospital roundabout, turn left along **Bar Lane**.

6. In 300 yards, when you reach the **A642 Aberford Road** roundabout, turn right, crossing Bar Lane, then use the pedestrian crossing to cross Aberford Road. Notice **Clarke Hall** to your right but take the footpath on your left, which runs down the side of the converted farm buildings. Follow this path with fields on your left and, after a while, with houses on your right.

7. In half a mile, at the end of the houses, bear left with the footpath, heading down towards **Stanley Ferry Flash**. When you arrive at the pool, at a bend on a track, cross the railway sleeper bridge and take the path through the metal kissing gate opposite. Continue with the next pool on your left.

8. Another kissing gate brings you to the **Aire and Calder Navigation**; turn left along the towpath. After passing **Ramsdens Bridge**, continue on the towpath but before you reach the **Stanley Ferry** pub take the ramp down into the car park and follow the driveway to **Ferry Lane**.

9. For a view of **Stanley Aqueduct** from the road bridge turn right, but otherwise cross Ferry Lane and follow the old railway walk, part of the **Trans-Pennine Trail**, for half a mile.

10. Cross **Aberford Road** (there's a crossing to the left if it's busy) and walk down **Lime Pit Lane** opposite to return to the start of this walk.

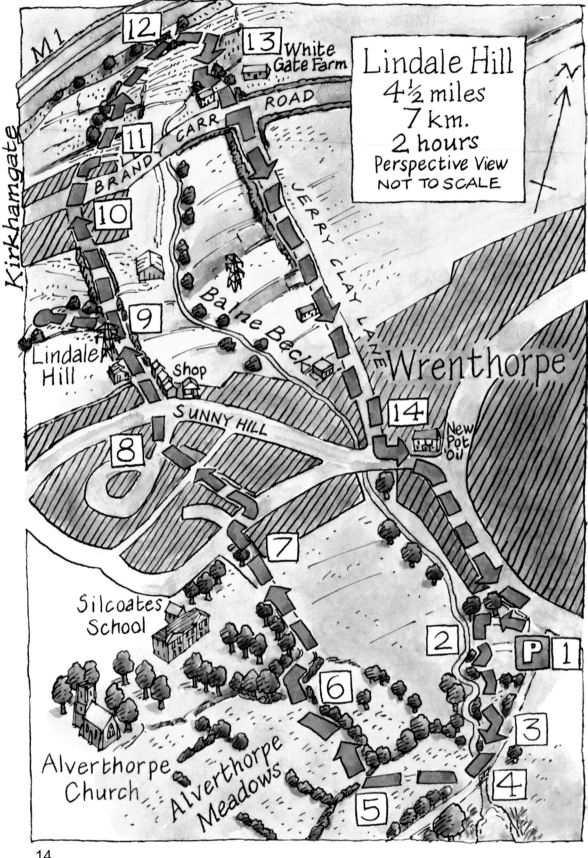

M1

12

13 White Gate Farm

BRANDY CARR ROAD

Lindale Hill
4½ miles
7 km.
2 hours
Perspective View
NOT TO SCALE

N

11

Kirkhangate

10

JERRY CLAY LANE

9

Barne Beck

Lindale Hill

Shop

Wrenthorpe

14

New Pot Oil

SUNNY HILL

8

7

Silcoates School

2

P 1

6

3

Alverthorpe Church

Alverthorpe Meadows

5

4

Lindale Hill

Parking: Wrenthorpe Park, Wrenthorpe Road (left turn just before the Bay Horse as you take the old Bradford Road out of Wakefield)
Buses: 100, 101, 103, 108, 481 and some 114s
OS ref.: SE 318223

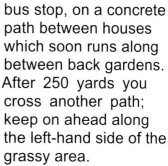

*Squeeze-stile,
Silcoates Lane*

1. From the car park, take the path that goes parallel to the road, down the right-hand side of the park towards **Balne Beck**.

2. Follow the tarmac path around until it turns back up the hill, then continue along the lower edge of the football pitch, with the stream on your right. Following the perimeter of the field, look out for a small path behind the goal posts which takes you on a small railway sleeper bridge across a small tributary stream. This brings you to a small meadow area. Again proceed with the stream on your right.

3. After crossing the small meadow, turn left to join the tarmac track then turn right along it.

4. After passing the balancing pond on your left, cross the footbridge and turn right, diagonally across the meadow towards a gap in the hedge.
When you get to the gap you'll see the tower of **Alverthorpe Church** *ahead of you. This is the most landlocked church in Yorkshire, equidistant from the North Sea and Irish Sea coastlines.*

5. Pass through this hedge by an old stile and continue with a mixed hedge (hawthorn, hazel, field maple and blackthorn) on your right.

6. Ignoring a small plank bridge on your right which takes you into a bushy wildlife area, continue on this path as it takes you into a copse. The path soon emerges to take you across the playing fields of **Silcoates School**.

7. Continue on the pavement alongside the car park on your right, then cross the drive to take the footpath which brings you out on **Silcoates Lane**. Turn right and in 50 yards turn left, just after the bus stop, on a concrete path between houses which soon runs along between back gardens. After 250 yards you cross another path; keep on ahead along the left-hand side of the grassy area.

8. When you emerge on **Sunnyhill Crescent**, turn right and cross the road then walk along **Lindale Lane**.

9. In quarter of a mile, immediately after the crest of the hill, as a farm comes into view on your right, take the path on the left to explore **Lindale Hill**. When you've taken a look around, return via the same path and turn left to continue your walk along **Lindale Lane**.

10. When you reach the end of the lane, cross **Brandy Carr Road** and take the public footpath **'to Woodhouse Lane'** ahead, via a crescent called **The Nooking**. After passing a brick-built house, take the footpath across the fields on your left.

11. Cross the small railway sleeper bridge and follow a hedgerow on your left for 300 yards. When you cross a ditch to enter the final field before the motorway, the path goes ahead of you towards the opposite corner of the field. This path might be difficult to see when there's a crop in the field but you're heading in the direction of a pylon, almost due north, on the other side of the motorway.

12. When you reach a track alongside the embankment, ignore the underpass beneath the motorway on your left and take the farm track on your right. The footpath strikes out to the right towards the outer corner of an adjacent field. Turn right and follow the field boundary on your left, now heading almost due south with the motorway behind you and **Lindale Hill** on the skyline ahead.

13. When you leave via the left-hand corner of this field, follow an old grassy tree-lined lane and in 300 yards, after

passing **White Gate Farm** on your left, turn left on **Brandy Carr Road**, then immediately right onto **Jerry Clay Lane**. There is no pavement alongside this country lane so walk facing oncoming traffic and take care on the blind summits.

14. In three quarters of a mile at the end of the lane, turn left onto **Wrenthorpe Lane** then, at the **New Pot 'Oil** public house, right along **Wrenthorpe Road** to return to the start of this walk.

Lindale Hill was once embanked around and used as a rabbit warren. On September 28th 1641, three labourers appeared in court in Wakefield charged with 'entering the warren, comonally called Lindale hill, belonging to Thomas, Earl Savile, and there killing with guns charged with powder and hail-shot two conies.'

Marine biologist **Charles Maurice Yonge** *(1899-1986)* was born far from the sea as his father **John Arthur Yonge** was headmaster at **Silcoates School** but in 1904 a 'Great Fire' resulted in the temporary exile of staff & pupils to Saltburn on the east coast. Perhaps this is where the young Maurice developed his fascination for marine life. As well as *The Sea Shore (1949)*, he wrote *A Year on the Barrier Reef (1930)* where he has a reef at Lizard Island named after him. He was awarded the Darwin Medal.

The school was founded in 1820 for the education of the sons of non-conformist clergymen. Its motto, *Clarior ex Ignibus* - 'all the brighter for the burning', refers to the Great Fire of 1904 .

Jerry Clay Lane

Rothwell

Rothwell Church dates from the 15th century but contains some Saxon carvings.

Railway walk

in **Carlton** you can visit a rhubarb-themed millennium green and a Rhubarb Triangle farm shop. Early in the year you can book a place on Oldroyd's Rhubarb Triangle Experience.

Carlton

'ROTHWELL is surrounded by collieries and stone quarries,' wrote **W.S. Banks** in 1871, 'It's other prominent trades are rope and band spinning and lucifer match making.' Seventy years later a visitor wrote 'The embattled church stands by an old pit-head, the coal now being brought up a mile away.'

It's much greener today: this walk follows the route of an old branch line, later part of the **East & West Yorkshire Union Railway**, which in January 1904 launched a passenger service to Stourton. Because of competition from the new electric tram this service ended after 8 months. **John Blenkinsop** *(1783-1831)* who designed the first practical steam locomotive, *The Salamanca*, for the Middleton Railway, is buried in the churchyard.

Small White butterfly on **Field Scabious**, railway walk.

Colliery spoil heap, now a rare sight, at **Robin Hood**.

17

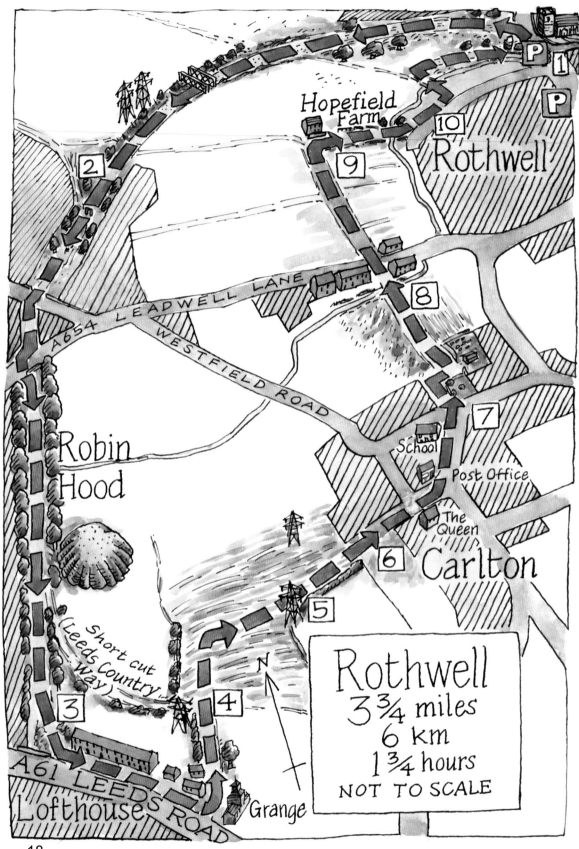

Hopefield Farm

10

Rothwell

9

A654 LEADWELL LANE

WESTFIELD ROAD

8

Robin
Hood

School

7

Post Office

Short cut
(Leeds Country
Way)

The
Queen

6

Carlton

5

N

3

4

Rothwell
3¾ miles
6 km
1¾ hours
NOT TO SCALE

A61 LEEDS ROAD

Lofthouse

Grange

2

Rothwell

Parking: car park opposite the church
Buses: 153, 444
OS ref.: SE 343282

1. Turn left out of the car park and, after you pass the church tower on your right, look out for a double flight of stone steps to your left. Climb these and follow the path to the right then turn left and go through the metal barrier which takes you onto a surfaced path which follows an old railway line. Keep to this surfaced path and ignore other tempting paths to the left and right.

2. After about a mile you pass a cul-de-sac of houses at **Robin Hood** on your left. Cross the track via the metal barriers and continue on the railway walk. After crossing a grassy area, cross a residential road, **Hopefield Drive**, straight ahead through the metal stile, then cross the busier A654 **Westfield Road** and continue the railway walk, diagonally opposite to the right, which now runs along the embankment.

3. After half a mile, when you come to the **A61 Leeds Road** at **Lofthouse**, walk up the slope on the left. Turn left and walk along the pavement for 300 yards then at **Lofthouse Grange/ Lofthouse Lodge Residential Homes**, 310 Leeds Road, turn left and take the footpath ahead.

4. After passing a pylon on your left, the path comes out at an open field. You need to head for the pylon on your right. Please follow any way-marking and, if necessary, make a short detour to avoid trampling the crops.

5. When you arrive at the pylon walk towards **Carlton** with the hedge on your right.

6. You pass **Shayfield Lane** recreation ground as you enter Carlton. Walk on ahead then turn left on **New Road** at the T junction by the post office.

7. After passing **Carlton Primary School** *(1875)*, on the junction of **New Road** and **Chapel**

Street, take the footpath ahead to the left of the small millennium park. The path soon turns to the right, around the back of the park, then left towards a terrace of houses on **Leadwell Lane**.

8. Cross Leadwell Lane and continue straight ahead towards **Hopefield Farm** (Oldroyd's) on the tarmac lane.

9. When you arrive at the farm, turn right on the footpath.

10. After crossing a concrete footbridge you emerge in **Rothwell** at a grassy ride. Turn left and, in 200 yards when you reach **Stone Brig Lane**, turn left on the public bridleway through **Rothwell Pastures** and cross two footbridges over the streams then turn right to return via the site of **John of Gaunt's Castle** and a short riverside path to the car park by the church.

John of Gaunt
Duke of Lancaster, 1340-1399

Thursday, 21 June, 1832: Wakefield antiquarian bookseller **John Cryer** visits Rothwell Church to see **Mr Gibson**, the parish clerk . . .

'He shewed me an old waist-coat without sleeves made of coarse canvas, several folds with wool be-tween, very thick and warm.' Cryer records in his journal.

It was originally the property of the famous **John of Gaunt**, Duke of Lancaster.

Formerly, when Mr Taylor was curate, we had some armour belonging to John of Gaunt, but he disposed of it to some one.

'Taylor was a queer fellow' wrote Cryer [1]

John of Gaunt at Rothwell?

In May 1359, John of Gaunt, fourth son of Edward III, married his cousin **Blanche** of Lancaster, and the couple came to live at the manor house at Rothwell.[2]

He hunted in the adjoining Park and it is said that he killed the last wild boar in these parts at Stye Bank near Rothwell.

After John's death on 3 February 1399, his nephew, the unpopular **Richard II**, sent his men to loot, break down fences and demolish the bridge from the manor to the church

But by 13 October John's eldest son was crowned **Henry IV**. The deposed King Richard died under mysterious circumstances in Pontefract Castle in February 1400.

A suit of Armour, 6ft 7inches tall, long *reputed* to be John of Gaunt's, can be seen in The Tower of London and you can still see that ancient Jack (sleeveless jacket) in Rothwell Church.

Robin Hood & John of Gaunt

Robert Hode - the Wakefield 'Robin Hood' (see my booklet *Walks in Robin Hood's Yorkshire*) - was made an outlaw after fighting at the **Battle of Boroughbridge**, 16 March 1322, for Blanche's great uncle, **Thomas Plantagenet, Earl of Lancaster**, then Lord of the Manor of Wakefield. Thomas was beheaded at Pontefract on 22 March but it seems that Robin was pardoned in December 1323 and was soon working in the household of **Edward II**, John of Gaunt's grandfather. John of Gaunt is credited with writing some of the early Robin Hood ballads. Blanche's brother-in-law **Geoffrey Chaucer** mentions the "hazellwood where Jolly Robin plaied" in his poem *Troilus and Criseyde* and in *The Deth of Blaunche* he features Blanche and a sorrowful knight, said to be John of Gaunt. John of Gaunt supported **Wycliffe** in the first full translation of the Bible into English.

[1]'A Defensive Garment in the Church of Rothwell, West Yorkshire' by Richard Knowles, Journal of the Arms and Armour Society, Vol. XI, no. 5, June 1985, p. 299-305; [2] History of Rothwell, 1877, John Batty, p. 119

The New Park

IN 1631 **Thomas Savile,** Lord of the Manor of Wakefield wrote in a letter 'Upon Tuesdaie I entend to kill a stagge in the Newe Park.'

The park, which was 6 miles in circuit, then contained about 220 fallow deer. During the middle ages poachers took deer, farmers broke down the fence to let their animals graze in the park and timber was removed by the cart load. Even a minister of the church was caught stealing green wood; in 1315 John, the Clerk of Horbury, was fined sixpence.

James Brudenell, 7th **Earl of Cardigan** *(1797-1868)* who led the Charge of the Light Brigade *(1854)* was owner of **Park Lodge Farm**, though he may never have visited it.

Even today you can see a ditch, once much deeper, and bank on stretches of the boundary. This barrier was topped with timber stakes or palings which gave the name to an outlying part of Ossett: **Paleside**. In the right light, you can make out the traces of medieval ridge-and-furrow strip cultivation in some of the adjacent pastures. Between points 11 & 13 this walk follows a medieval highway from Woodkirk.

From 1894 to 1900 sub-postmaster and chemist **John. W. Cussons** *(1867-1922)* had his premises in Station Road, Ossett. The town's 1893 *Cockburn's Directory* includes an advertisement for **Cussons Compound Rhubarb Pills**. His initials can still be seen in a decorative carving on what is now the Yorkshire Bank. Cussons left Ossett to become a manufacturing chemist making Imperial Leather soap.

Bushey Beck was once called the Humble Jumble. The Viking word 'Humul' meant a stone or boulder, 'jumble' a rough, bushy hollow. In the early nineteenth century, the beck was dammed in two places known as Mr Fenton's Upper and Lower ponds. A waterwheel was used to operate a pump which de-watered Fenton's coal mines in the New Park. In 1798 both Fenton and rival mine-owner Smithson at Low Laithes opened railways to staiths on the Calder at Wakefield.

Fenton's railway used bullocks as pulling power, while Smithson's, running parallel to it, used horse power.

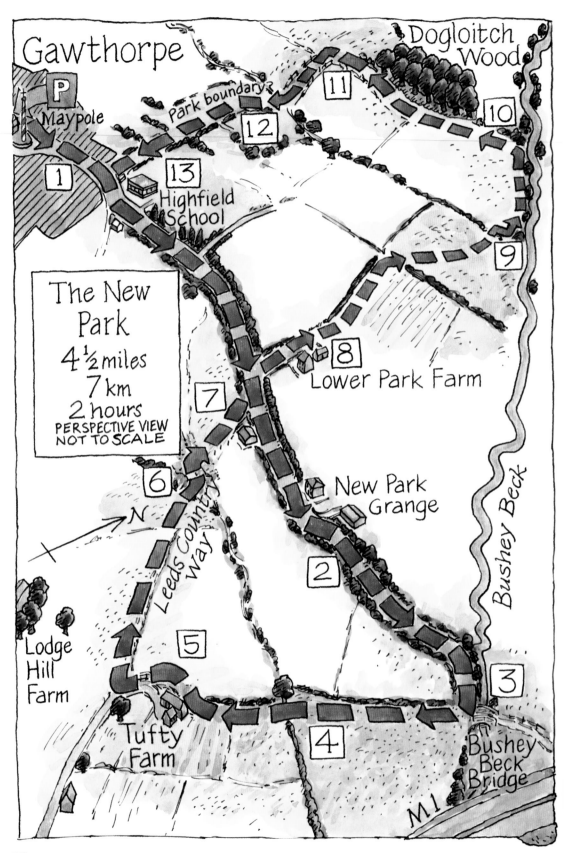

Gawthorpe

P

Maypole

1

Park boundary

11

12

Dogloitch Wood

10

13

Highfield School

9

The New Park
4½ miles
7 km
2 hours
PERSPECTIVE VIEW
NOT TO SCALE

8

Lower Park Farm

7

New Park Grange

N

6

Leeds Country Way

2

Bushey Beck

Lodge Hill Farm

5

3

Tufty Farm

4

Bushey Beck Bridge

M1

The New Park

Parking: car park, Cross Street, Gawthorpe
Buses: 117, 119, 120 **OS ref.:** SE 273221

1. Turn right out of the car park and, with the **Shoulder of Mutton** public house on your left, walk down **High Street**. After 500 yards you pass **Highfield School** on your left and continue ahead on the tarmac lane (**Gawthorpe Lane**) .

2. Continue on this lane for half a mile and, after you pass **New Park Grange Farm** on your right and **New Park Grange** on your left, take the bridleway between hedges to the right as the track swings to the left towards some rhubarb sheds.

3. Just before you come to **Bushey Beck Bridge**, a small stone bridge on a bend in the track, turn right along the public footpath on the right-hand side of the field, with the hedge on your right.

4. At the far corner of the field turn left then immediately right by the willow to continue along the right-hand side of the next field. As you ascend the slope you pass the buildings of **Tufty Farm** on your left.

5. When you join the driveway to the farm, follow it up the hill and in 60 yards, as the lane turns to the left by an ash tree, turn sharp right on the footpath to Gawthorpe 1¼. This follows the right-hand boundary of the field and then, when the hedge ends it continues in the same direction across the next field.

6. Cross the stile and follow the path which turns to the left, then right, to cross a footbridge. You soon pass a metal gate on your right and, keeping the field boundary on your right, make your way up the slope towards **Gawthorpe Lane**, in the top right corner of the field adjacent to **New Park Grange Farm**. *Beware*; there's a surprisingly deep ditch hidden amongst the vegetation to your right! A timber bridge over a deep stone-lined ditch takes you back onto Gawthorpe Lane.

7. Turn left on the lane and then immediate right towards **Lower Park Farm**, on a track to West Ardsley 1¼.*(Or return directly to Gawthorpe and save the second and longer leg of this walk for another day).*

8. After passing the farm buildings on your right, go through the gate into the field and keep the hedge on your left. At the far left-hand corner cross into the next field. The path goes at about 45 degrees down to the right across the field.

9. A stile and bridge take you into the next field. Turn right down towards the stream then turn to continue with the stream on your right.

10. When you get to the far right corner swing round up the hill keeping the hedge on your right towards **Dogloitch Wood**, ignoring the footpath which goes over the plank bridge on your right.

Oaks, birch and hazel grow in the wood with wood sage at the edges. The flowers of creeping *thistle on this sheltered, sunny side of the wood attract **speckled wood, peacock, red admiral, comma, gatekeeper, small copper,** and **green-veined white** butterflies in summer.*

11. Follow the track alongside the wood and, after you've passed the last of the trees, turn left along a grassy farm track. In 250 yards cross a concrete bridge into the next field (the plank footbridge appears to have fallen into disrepair).

12. Continue up the slope ahead with the hedge on your left.

For the next half mile you are following the western boundary of the medieval deer park (see page 21).

13. After a stile and a narrow footpath you emerge at the side of Rooks Nest, no. 99 High Street. Turn right

to return to the start of the walk.

Maypole, Gawthorpe

Rhubarb Bread & Butter Pudding

serves 6

6 slices good quality white
    bread approximately
    1cm thick
softened butter
5 dessertspoons rhubarb &
    ginger jam
250g diced fresh rhubarb
3 medium eggs
280ml whole milk
85ml double cream
85g caster sugar

Rhubarb triangles - in this case rhubarb & ginger jam sandwiches - are the starting point for this pudding which combines the golden crunchiness of the bread & butter with the fruity piquancy of the diced baked rhubarb.

Butter the 6 slices of bread then spread 3 of them with the jam and sandwich together. Spread the top of each sandwich with butter. Cut each sandwich into quarters then each quarter in half diagonally so you end up with small triangular sandwiches.

Lightly butter an ovenproof dish then place the sandwiches in it and scatter the chopped rhubarb on top of them.

Whisk together the eggs, milk, cream and sugar then pour over the bread and rhubarb.

Bake at 190°C for about 30 minutes or until set. Serve with crème fraîche, cream or custard.

Rhubarb to Rhubarb

Thornes Park to Horbury

Thornes Flood Lock Bridge

Pony at Dudfleet.

Dudfleet Lane

Lupset golf course

*Horbury: sprouting rhubarb carved in locally grown oak by **Handspring Design** of Sheffield.*

IT'S SURPRISING how much open space and open water there is between Wakefield and Horbury, which run together when you travel by road. Engineer **John Smeaton** *(1724-1792)* used construction tackle that he'd used in building the Eddystone lighthouse when he started work on making the River Calder navigable upstream from Wakefield in 1758 but the Horbury Cut of the **Calder and Hebble Navigation** didn't open until 1838. By then railways were changing the landscape and **George Stephenson** *(1781-1848)*, was engineer for this stretch of the **Manchester and Leeds Railway** which opened in 1840. This was the first trans-Pennine rail route.

A house on Thornes Lane, diagonally opposite the Rhubarb sculpture, bears the date 1839. It was built using stone excavated during the making of a tunnel at Horbury. As you can see when you reach Dudfleet Lane, further excavations incorporated the tunnel into the quarter mile long **Addingford Cutting**.

The 240ft **motorway bridge** across the Calder opened in October 1968 and stands as a monument to 4 construction workers who lost their lives when two of the 30ft long, 250 ton sections of the bridge collapsed. The **Sustrans** cycle route opened in 2005.

Rhubarb sculpture, Thornes Park.

Duck pond, Thornes Park.

Riverside path, Horbury Junction

Thornes Pump base

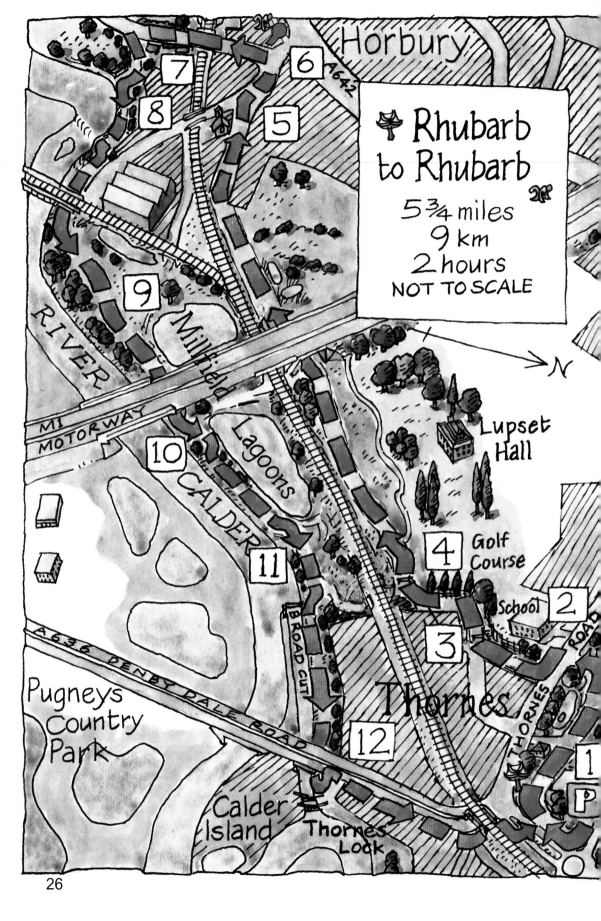

Rhubarb to Rhubarb

Parking: Holmfield Park car park by roundabout at junction of Thornes Lane and the A636 Denby Dale Road, **Thornes**, Wakefield   **Buses:** 119, 120, 128, 265, 435, 443   **OS ref.:** SE 328196

1. Facing the round-about, turn right on the footpath/cycleway along the edge of the park. Note the **rhubarb sculpture** at the junction with **Thornes Road** but continue on the path through the park, passing the **duck pond**.

2. When you come to the **Rose Garden**, turn left and leave the park via the iron gates. Cross **Thornes Road** (there's a pedestrian crossing on your right), turn left and take the footpath on your right alongside the fence of the **Cathedral School**.

3. When you reach **Thornes Moor Road**, turn right on the **cycleway** signed 'Horbury 2'.

4. Keep on the cycleway for a mile, passing through 'Echo Tunnel' under the motorway and eventually reaching **Green Lane**, Horbury.

5. At the end of Green Lane turn right and follow **Daw Lane** to the **rhubarb sculpture** and welcome bench on the verge by the **A642**.

6. Turn around and go back down Daw Lane for 100 yards and take the first turn, **Dudfleet Lane**, on your right.

7. After crossing a bridge over the railway, ignore the first public footpath (to 'Millfield Road ¼ mile') on your left then, immediately after you pass **Castle Hill Farm** on your left, turn left on a footpath which follows the perimeter fence of the **Waste Water Treatment Works** on your right.

8. In 250 yards turn left on the riverside path then, in a further 250 yards as you pass the weir, turn right on the cycleway/footpath. You pass **Charles Roberts Office Park** on your left, then go under the rail-way bridge, ignoring the wooden steps to the 'dark passage' across the river. Continue on the riverside path ahead.

9 Make your way across a wide grassy area heading towards the right-hand end of the motorway, with **Millfield Lagoon** on your left.

10. When you pass under the motorway bridge, continue on the rutted track with the next lagoon on your left. As an alternative to the track, after about 50 yards look for a small path which takes you up onto the riverside flood embankment.

11. After crossing the sluice gates at the end of the lagoon keep on the track that runs parallel to the riverbank. In 300 yards, when you reach **Thornes Flood Lock Bridge** on your right, make your way up to the bridge and walk along the towpath for half a mile.

12. You pass under the road then, just before you get to **Thornes Lock***, turn left up the ramp then right alongside the **A636 Denby Dale Road**, keeping to this side of the road. After you've passed the base of **Thornes Pump** and gone beneath the railway bridge, cross the road at the pedestrian crossings to return to the start of this walk.

*There are rhubarb fields further along this path.

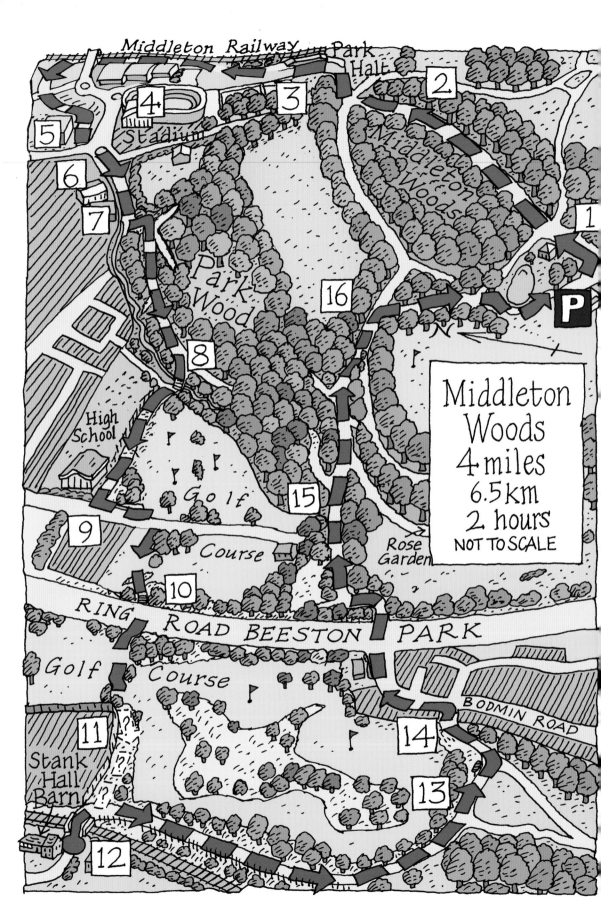

Middleton Woods

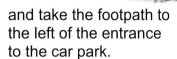
Middleton Park lake

Parking: Middleton Park lake car park, off Town Street
Buses: 9, 13, 74, 481. John Charles Centre for Sport; 481
OS ref.: SE 300286

1. Walk away from the lake to the top end of the car park and turn left on the tarmac driveway. Pass the visitor centre on your left and continue ahead, ignoring tracks to the right and left. You soon find yourself on a long, straight stretch of lane going down through the woods.

2. As the track bends to the left at the bottom of the slope, ignore turns back into the wood on your left and bear right with the track to pass between two large stone gateposts. Continue through the squeeze-stile at the side of the metal gate then cross the track and take the wide path ahead. In 100 yards turn left to **Park Halt**, the end of the **Middleton Railway**.

3. Walk along the platform and continue on

Park Halt

the footpath ahead with the railway on your right and the sports fields on your left.

4. When you reach the buildings of the **John Charles Centre for Sport**, keep on the narrow path alongside the railway. **Beware of the trains!**

5. Immediately after passing under a concrete road bridge, follow the path as it curves to the left up a slope. After crossing another track, continue on a track which runs along at the foot of the road embankment back towards the stadium.

6. Another squeeze stile brings you out at the far side of the stadium. Cross the road ahead

and take the footpath to the left of the entrance to the car park.

7. A broad path takes you into **Park Wood** along the backs of several industrial units. In a quarter of a mile, by the last of the industrial units, turn left to take the path up past lumps and hollows on your right to a meeting of woodland tracks. Turn right on the main track and continue on it for a quarter of a mile through Park Wood.

8. Ignore the first path down to the stream but,

as the valley narrows to a gully, at a Y-junction take the path on your right down to the stream. Cross the footbridge and go through the kissing gate out of the wood then turn left on an old cobbled path with the

spiked metal fence of **Cockburn High School** on your right and, after a short distance, a golf course on your left.

9. When you come out on **Gipsy Lane**, turn left and walk up the driveway through the gates of the golf club, then, after 50 yards or so, take the public footpath 'to Stank Hall Barn' on your right. There is waymarking but in 200 yards it's easy to miss the footpath when it crosses a golfer's path before going down steps through dense bushes to bring you out abruptly on the busy **Ring Road Beeston Park**.

10. Cross the road and climb another set of steps up through dense bushes. The path then follows a narrow belt of

30

trees and bushes across the golf course. You start with the trees on your left but you'll need to go through the second of two of the openings to end up with the trees on your right and fairway on your left.

11. Now comes the trickiest part of this walk; keeping to the right-hand boundary of the golf course, make your way as best you can to the far right-hand corner. The Ordnance Survey map and way-markers on the ground confirm that the right of way follows the fence along the back of the houses of **Park Wood Crescent** but at the moment this route is blocked by brambles and a fence at the far end. You need to find a safe way around this obstruction to the foot-path and you will probably find yourself descending a grassy, scrubby bank. _Beware of the narrow ditch!_

12. When you arrive at the footpath alongside the fence at the side of the Wakefield to Leeds railway turn left _(or turn right to view **Stank Hall Barn**)_ and follow the path with the fence on

your right for almost half a mile.

13. When you emerge at a meadow turn left on the winding path. This swings up to the left into a shallow cutting.

14. When you come out on **Bodmin Road**, turn left and, in 200 yards at the T-junction, cross the road and take the track, **Balcliffe Lane**, part of the Middleton Heritage Trail. This track swings round to the left with a golf course to your right.

15. Continue on this surfaced path, bearing right towards Wood Pit at a junction and ignoring smaller paths to the left and right, and in half a mile when you meet a driveway, follow it to the left.

16. In 200 yards, at two large horse chestnut trees, turn right in the direction of the visitor centre. This brings you back up to the lake and the car park beyond.

Stank Hall Barn, Beeston, is a scheduled Ancient Monument. It's said to date from 1420 with a phase of rebuilding in 1492. It was originally covered in wattle-and-daub.

2009

Middleton Woods

The stone building attached to the barn on the left is said to have been used as a chapel by **Major Joshua Greathead** *(1616-1684)*, a roundhead who led his own squadron and fought at the battle of Adwalton Moor in 1644. At the time Stank Hall Farm belonged to the Royalist John Hodgson.

After the Restoration, Greathead, alias 'the Ironmonger' and described as a 'cunning knaveish man', became involved in the Puritan **Farnley Wood Plot** to attack Leeds on 12th October 1663. His reputation appears to have drawn local farmers into the plot but Greathead himself turned government informer. The attack was aborted but on 14 January, 1664, three of the conspirators, convicted of treason, were hung, drawn and quartered on a specially constructed gallows at Chapeltown Moor, an event which drew record crowds to Leeds.

Peter Mason, a local joiner, acted as executioner and had the job of preparing the three heads overnight so that they could be set on spikes at the Moot Hall in Briggate. The heads remained in place for 13 years until they were then blown down in a storm.

Middleton Railway, the first founded by Act of Parliament in 1758, became the first to successfully use steam locomotives in 1812.

'The steam engine lately invented by Mr. Blenkinsop, agent at the colliery of Charles Brandling, esquire, near Leeds . . . conveys above twenty waggons loaded with coals from the pits to Leeds. By two of these machines constantly employed the labour of at least fourteen horses is saved.'

George Walker, 1814

Colliery at Middleton, George Walker, 1814

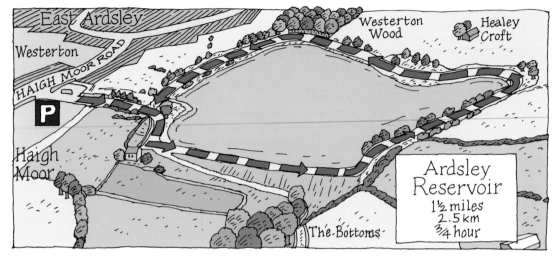

East Ardsley
Westerton Wood
Healey Croft
Westerton
HAIGH MOOR ROAD
P
Haigh Moor
The Bottoms

Ardsley Reservoir
1½ miles
2.5 km
¾ hour

Ardsley Reservoir

Parking: Yorkshire Water car park, Haigh Moor Road
Buses: 114, 117, 153, 205 **OS ref.:** SE 286249

Here's an easy walk that you can fit in even if you've got only an hour to spare. It's a level waterside circuit but from the embankment there's a panorama over New Park with the spire of Holy Trinity, Ossett, Emley Moor mast and the Pennines beyond. Completed in 1887, this is a holding reservoir for Wakefield's water supply, piped from reservoirs in the Pennines above Ripponden. Rare gulls - including Iceland and glaucous - have been spotted amongst commoner species roosting here.

I'm grateful to **Yorkshire Water** and **KeyLand Developments** for allowing me to include this walk. The directions couldn't be simpler; from the car park, head towards the reservoir and follow the perimeter path around it.

East Ardsley Church, away from the rest of the village, was a favourite target of the body-snatchers or 'Resurrectionists'. Under cover of darkness they would enter the churchyard to dig up newly buried corpses. These were sold to the medical schools in London and Edinburgh for about £10 each.

In November 1831 a well organised gang, masterminded by John Craig Hodgson, an articled clerk of Leeds, stole a body from the graveyard. It was later found on the overnight Leeds to Edinburgh Courier coach in a box marked 'To be left until called for, Glass, and keep this side up.'

The whole gang were brought to trial.